THE HOME FRONT

A Revue with Sketches

Lynn Brittney

Published by Playstage
United Kingdom.

An imprint of Write Publications Ltd

www.playsforadults.com

Designed by Kate Lowe, Greensands Graphics
Printed by Creeds Ltd, Bridport, Dorset

Note to producers about staging "The Home Front"

Although the piece, according to the number of pages in the script, looks quite short, by the time the songs have been sung (usually with a repeat of the lyrics given) and the sound effects during blackouts have been added in, the piece should run a respectable hour and a half plus whatever time is taken for the interval. There is also the possibility of adding an audience participation sing-along at the end, as part of the curtain calls, should a drama group wish to do so.

SET

As this is a review, very little is required in the way of a set. Those pieces outlined in the script are representational and could be substituted by other things but the radio image in Act 1 and the American flag and London Underground symbol in Act II are ideal, as they are relevant to the dramatic content of the script.

Extra set dressing could be added, such as WWII posters on side flats (see SOURCES below).

The furniture for the sketches could be brought on by the actors in the blackout of by members of the review. The pieces required are fairly basic wooden kitchen furniture.

COSTUME

Costume should, obviously, be of the period, as outlined in the script. It would be ideal if a pianist, in costume, could accompany the songs from the side or in front of the stage. Otherwise, it is suggested that the accompaniment is recorded and controlled by technicians.

PERFORMANCE

For those actors who are reading the articles; radio broadcasts and reminiscences for the review portion of the show, it would be ideal if a variety of accents could be used, ranging from posh to cockney and other regional dialects, as the script suggests in the locations of the reminiscences. The family in the sketches are working class Londoners. Some American accents feature in the review and the sketches.

Some of the actors in the review can read from notebooks, or from sheets of paper, as radio announcers would, but those who are "reminiscing" should do so from memory.

The WOMAN's VOICE on the radio is most effectively done via an offstage microphone. It could be pre-recorded but there is the complication of other actors speaking in between the radio broadcast. The MAN with the mouth organ, at the end of the play, could mime to a pre-recorded piece if the actor is unable to actually play the mouth organ.

SOURCES OF SOUND EFFECTS AND OTHER MATERIAL

The Imperial War Museum www.iwmshop.org.uk/index.html.

For Churchill's speeches; Blitz sound effects; posters; WWII music CDs; replica newspapers.

Sound Effects Library.com www.sound-effects-library.com

For BBC sound effects and others; bombing; airplanes; air raid sirens; anti-aircraft guns.

Amazon.co.uk or Music Exchange www.music-exchange.co.uk or any local printed music/instrument shop for WWII songbooks and sheet music

THE HOME FRONT

CAST *(In order of appearance)*

FOR THE REVIEW:

Six Singers	any combination of men and women.
Ist Man	also take the parts of AMERICAN REPORTER,
2nd Man	AMERICAN SOLDIER, WARDEN and MAN
3rd Man	playing mouth organ. Plus assorted people at the end of the play.
1st Woman	also take the parts of WOMAN's VOICE on the
2nd Woman	radio and Blitz victims/helpers at the end of the
3rd Woman	play.

NOTE: SINGERS and MEN and WOMEN can double up if necessary.

CAST *(In order of appearance)*

FOR THE SKETCHES:

MUM	mother of VI's husband, living with her daughter-in-law, obsessed with knitting, aged 65 – 75.
DAD	father of VI's husband, living with his daughter' in-law, veteran of WW1, aged 65-75.
VI	long-suffering wife of Big Charlie, a professional thief, now serving in the Army, aged 45+.
DORIS	VI's 18 year old daughter.
ROSE	VI's 20 year old daughter.

SID	a spiv. Went to school with VI and is sweet on her, excused military service for a heart condition.
WOMAN on the radio	posh BBC voice, reading out a recipe.
GEORGE	American soldier, aged 35-45
JOE	American soldier, barely out of his teens.
ARP WARDEN	(see REVIEW cast list) aged 50+
MAN with mouth organ	(see REVIEW cast list) aged 50+

NOTE: GEORGE and JOE could be REVIEW cast members doubling, if necessary. In fact, all of the SKETCH cast members could double as singers, if required.

The action of the sketches takes place in VI's kitchen.

THE HOME FRONT

The stage is bare, except for a large image of a 1940s radio upstage centre. There are two large 1940s radio microphones on stands either side of the down stage area. Spotlights are trained on the radio image and the two microphones.

The "V for Victory" drumbeat is heard.

(Then six people (men and women), THE SINGERS, come out and stand three to a microphone. The introduction is played – they all salute and sing "There'll always be an England.")

THERE'LL ALWAYS BE AN ENGLAND – lyrics

There'll always be an England
While there's a country lane
Wherever there's a cottage small
Beside a field of grain.
There'll always be an England
While there's a busy street
Wherever there's a turning wheel
A million marching feet.
Red, white and blue
What does it mean to you?
Surely you're proud, shout it out loud
Britons awake.
The Empire too,
We can depend on you
Freedom remains, these are the chains nothing can break.

There's always be an England
And England shall be free
If England means as much to you
As England means to me.

(THE SINGERS march off)

(1ST MAN enters and speaks into one of the microphones)

1ST MAN   Mr Chamberlain's broadcast was not impressive. I remembered him from the newsreels, coming out of his aeroplane after Munich, waving his little piece of paper and promising 'peace in our time.' I thought he looked like a sheep, and now he bleated like a sheep. He talked about notes being sent and replies not being received. He regretted that a state of war existed between Great Britain and Germany. He sounded really hurt, like Hitler was some shiftless council tenant who had failed to pay his rent after faithfully promising to do so.

That wasn't the way to talk to Hitler; he should be threatening to kick his teeth in....I knew there'd be trouble....

There was. The sirens went immediately. We didn't know what to do. We had no shelters; nothing but little gas masks in cardboard boxes. We went to the front windows and stared out. Everything was peaceful and sunny. Old Charlie Harris, who hadn't worked for years with his bad chest, after being gassed on the Somme, was marching round the square sticking his chest out. Wearing his best suit and medals from the Last Lot. He looked determined but ridiculous. Mum said he had volunteered to be a warden yesterday, and obviously felt he should do something.

Dad said ' If he sounds his rattle, that means poison gas - put your gas mask on.'

I said 'But he hasn't got a rattle.'

There wasn't a cloud in the sky - let alone a German bomber. My old teddy bear was sitting in the corner. I hadn't spared him a glance in years, but now he looked at me appealingly. I put him under my bed for safety.

Then the all-clear sounded.

Charlie Brown headed straight home for a strong cup of tea.

(1ST MAN exits and 1ST WOMAN enters to take up position at the other microphone)

1ST WOMAN   My father got a copy of the Daily Express war map, which we hung on the kitchen wall and decorated with little coloured flags representing the Allied and German forces. It was good fun – but quite unreal. As unreal as the popular songs on the wireless...

(1ST WOMAN is joined by THE SINGERS at the two microphones. Intro is played and then they sing "The Seigfried Line")

THE SEIGFRIED LINE – lyrics

We're going to hang out the washing on the Siegfried Line
Have you any dirty washing, Mother dear?
We're going to hang out the washing on the Siegfried Line
For the washing day is here.
Whether the weather may be wet or fine,
We will hang it out, without a care.
We're going to hang out the washing on the Siegfried Line
If the Siegfried Line's still there! *(repeat)*

*(THE SINGERS and 1ST WOMAN leave and 2ND
WOMAN enters, taking up position at the microphone. She
reads from a piece of paper.)*

2ND WOMAN   A message from the Minister of Health.

All over the country the local authorities, at my request, are
preparing to make a survey of available housing
accommodation, as part of our plans for transferring
children and others, in an emergency, to the homes of those
who are willing to take care of them. I hope that every
householder will give all possible help to the visitors making
the survey. Some of them will be officers of the local
authorities and some of them will be volunteer helpers.
They will be going round to collect the information which
we need, in order that we in Whitehall may estimate how
many people could be properly accommodated without
overcrowding either guests or hosts.

If an emergency should come upon us we shall have the
greatest need of the help of voluntary workers, such as
members of the Women's Institutes, in the country districts
to which the children will be sent. It is an immense
undertaking to move and re-settle even one million people -
especially when they are children. There will have to be an
infinite number of special arrangements - for communal
cooking and feeding, perhaps for communal laundry work,
for crèches and play centres and any other activities. This
can only be done if there are willing helpers remaining in
the districts to which the children will be sent, and it is for
this reason that the services which the women can give -
both as householders looking after children from the danger
areas in their own homes and as workers engaged in these

thousand and one community tasks - must rank as national service of the first importance.

(2ND WOMAN stays where she is and 3RD WOMAN enters and takes up position at the opposite microphone. She has a notebook and pen and adopts the tone of a female reporter. 2ND WOMAN reacts to her news.)

3RD WOMAN   London children evacuated to Norfolk are reported to have put on half a stone in a week.

A housewife in the Ipswich district who is able to feed her two young guests for eleven shillings a week intends to spend the extra six shillings she is receiving on boots and winter clothes for them.

Hundreds of fathers and mothers from the evacuation areas are visiting their children in the reception districts - by train, bus, car and bicycle. Will this social upheaval, one wonders, be the beginning of a serious back-to-the land movement?

(Both women exit and there is temporarily a bare stage. A few bars of "Stars and Stripes Forever" play and an AMERICAN REPORTER comes out to one of the microphones. He is wearing a sharp suit and hat at a rakish angle.)

AMERICAN
REPORTER   This is Frederick Marshall – correspondent of the United Press of America in London.

I just want to reassure the British that Americans DO care.

During the first eight months of the war, Americans imagined the conflict to be a pantomime rather than an honest-to-God struggle between two worlds. They fancied the German and Allied armies grimacing at one another from Seigfried to Maginot lines. Peace rumours chased each other through American newspapers, and it was widely believed that a group of influential British appeasers would momentarily step into the daylight to conclude a makeshift peace with Germany. Suspicion that the war was an imposture explains why American voluntary relief trickled to Europe sparingly, totalling only seventy thousand pounds from September 1939 to May 1940.

America's attitude changed suddenly after Denmark, Norway, Holland, Belgium and France were crushed under the Nazi war machine, and especially when German bombers began to wreak destruction and death in Britain. Talk of appeasement and the phoney war stopped. Millions of Americans ceased taking a box-office view of the struggle and sensed that their own fate is tied to British victory or defeat. While munitions and aeroplanes started streaming across the Atlantic, United States voluntary help in the war's second eight months rose to three million pounds to which more than fifteen million Americans contributed. About eighty percent of this relief flowed through the American Red Cross.

Neither Germany or Italy has received any American Red Cross assistance, however. On the day war was declared, the American Red Cross approached all Europe's Red Cross societies but the Germans said they needed no American help. When Italy entered the war on June 10, she replied similarly. It was news of Dunkirk and of the army returning without medical stores that first loosed the big flood of American aid. Then came the story of thirty thousand Channel Islanders, homeless in Britain – and of evacuated Gibraltarians, of Poles, and fugitive French fleeing to Cornwall in tiny open boats. But it was the unleashing of air war over Britain in August and the tales of British courage and successful RAF defiance that dispelled the last doubt that this war is a deadly challenge to ideals which Americans, too, hold dear.

Thousands of Americans proved their own earnestness by giving their blood. There were six thousand blood donors in New York City alone. The first blood plasma was flown to Britain in August – in September and October, three thousand gallons a month were being sent – each gallon sufficient for four transfusions.

Medical aid from America ranges from one hundred and fifty six ambulances – three hundred more are being shipped as I speak – to three hundred thousand blankets, over fifteen thousand surgical dressings, ten x-ray units, over one hundred thousand hospital garments and vast quantities of pharmaceutical drugs.

American businessmen in Britain collected one hundred thousand pounds in a week and presented over a hundred American-made ambulance units to the Ministry of Health and America's Junior Red Cross sent Christmas presents for two hundred and ten thousand British children.

So folks, please remember, your friends in America do care.

(AMERICAN REPORTER exits to sounds of "Stars and Stripes Forever". BLACKOUT. VOICE OF WINSTON CHURCHILL on the radio.)

BROADCAST OF WINSTON CHURCHILL	... What General Weygand has called the Battle of France is over. The Battle of Britain is about to begin. Upon this battle depends the survival of Christian civilisation. Upon it depends our own British life, and the long continuity of our constitutions and our Empire. The whole fury and might of the enemy must very soon be turned on us.

(Halfway through this speech the lights come up to show MUM and DAD seated at a kitchen table listening to the broadcast. MUM is knitting – something she does continuously throughout the War. The speech continues.)

Hitler knows that he will have to break us in this island or lose the war. If we can stand up to him all Europe may be freed and the life of the world may move forward into broad, sunlit uplands. But if we fail then the whole world, including the United States, including all that we have known and cared for, will sink into the abyss of a new dark age, made more sinister, and perhaps more protracted, by the lights of perverted science.

Let us therefore brace ourselves to our duty, and so bear ourselves that if the British Empire and its Commonwealth last for a thousand years, men will still say, ' This was their finest hour'. "

(The National Anthem plays. DAD stands up to attention; MUM carries on knitting and VI enters, in her hat and coat, carrying a roll of blackout material. She switches off the radio in mid-anthem)

DAD   *(horrified)* 'Ere! That's sacrilege that is!

VI	Oh come off it Dad. They play the National Anthem about eight hundred times a day on the radio at the moment. You'll wear your legs out bobbing up and down like that.
MUM	Young Charlie got off all right, did 'e?
VI	Yeah. 'E was alright. Cheeky little beggar. I 'ope they can cope with 'im where 'e's going.
MUM	It's going to be quiet in this house now Big Charlie's gone and volunteered and little Charlie's been evacuated.
VI	Mum, for the last time – Big Charlie did not volunteer! 'E didn't 'ave any choice. The judge said it was the army or Pentonville. At least now we'll 'ave some regular money coming in. And – yes – it will be quiet round 'ere. With little Charlie gone as well, it means we won't be 'aving a visit from the coppers every other day.
DAD	Yes...well. I still don't see why you 'ad to send the lad away. I mean 'e's not a child anymore, 'e's twelve years old.
VI	Because 'e was a right little chip off the old block, that's why. 'E's going to a nice little village with a village bobby to keep an eye on 'im. I'm not 'aving a son of mine getting up to all sorts in London when the bombing starts. 'E's better off out of it. Is there any tea left in the pot?
MUM	Yes, love. Best make the most of it, Vi. Ration books arrived today.
VI	Mm. 'Ere you are, Dad. *(gives him the blackout material)* You can make yourself useful. All this stuff needs to be nailed to the window upstairs.
DAD	'Ere! I did my lot in the last war, you know.
VI	Yes, well you'll 'ave to do a bit more in this one, won't

you? Seeing as you're the only man left in the 'ouse now.

(DAD exits grumbling. VI sits down and pours herself a cup of tea.)

MUM   'E's got the 'ump because the paper says they ain't going to 'ave an Armistice Day Parade at the Cenotaph this year, 'E was looking forward to meeting 'is old comrades.

VI   Looking forward to getting a skinful you mean.

MUM   Not going to be any Bonfire Night neither. Shame really.

VI   Well, we got to make the best of it, Mum. Dad'll 'ave to start on the back garden this week. Government says we should plant veg everywhere and that's what we're going to do.

MUM   Well at least they've let us 'ave our full coal ration again. I was worried 'ow we was going to get through this winter.

VI   Oh don't worry Mum. This war won't last long. The Germans 'ave 'ad one go at knocking off Herr Hitler, they're bound to make a better job of it sooner or later.

(DORIS and ROSE enter – aged 18 and 20 respectively. DORIS is excited.)

DORIS   'Ere Mum, guess what? I just got the last two pairs of Lisle stocking at Cheesemans. I 'ad to queue for an 'our and 'alf, but I got them. Cost me 'alf me wages but at least I'll be warm this winter.

VI   Oh yes? And where's the 'ousekeeping money? Are you going to go without food while you're keeping warm? Cos I'm sure I can't afford to feed a lady of fashion who doesn't pay 'er way.

DORIS   Oh Mum! I'll give you double next week, I promise. But I just 'ad to 'ave 'em, didn't I?

VI   What about Rose? Did she get some?

ROSE   *(sulkily)* No I didn't. I didn't know they was on sale. By the time I got there, they was all gone. She always gets whatever's going.

                (SID the spiv enters, carrying a large canvas bag over his shoulder.)

SID   Hello, hello. Did I hear the sound of a lady in distress?

EVERYONE   Hullo Sid etc.

VI   I'll make fresh tea. D'you want a cup, Sid?

SID   Never refuse your hospitality, Vi. You know I've always been sweet on you. I shall 'ave to watch myself now though, won't I Ma? Now that Big Charlie's gawn away. Don't want the neighbours talking.

VI   Huh! Big Charlie was 'ardly ever 'ere – even when there wasn't a war on.

MUM   Now Vi! I won't 'ear you making remarks like that about my son when 'e's not 'ere to defend 'imself. 'Ow come you've not joined up then Sid? Got to do your bit for your country, you know.

SID   I tried, Ma. Believe me I tried. Wouldn't 'ave me you see. On account of my dodgy 'eart.

VI   Dodgy 'eart?!

MUM   I didn't know you was an invalid Sid.

VI   No neither did I. Nor did 'alf the women whose back walls you've jumped over, either.

SID   'Ere now – Saucy! You'll get me a bad reputation, won't she ma? I 'ave to admit that I was not aware that I 'ad a dodgy ticker until I went for me army medical. Told me right off they did. Mr Potts, they said, we appreciate you offering your services for your country but we must regretfully decline, on account of the fact that your 'eart is not strong enough to face combat.

MUM Well I never.

(SID liberally spoons sugar into his tea and stirs it)

ROSE *(sarcastically)* Sugar good for a bad 'eart, is it?

VI Don't be so cheeky Rose!

SID No. Fair do's. Rose is right to point out my wastefulness. Let me give you a little present to make amends.

(He fishes in his bag and brings out a bag of sugar and three pairs of stockings.)

ROSE Stockings! *(She goes to grab them)*

VI 'Ere. 'ere! Mind your manners Rose. I'm not too old to appreciate 'aving nice looking legs too. Give us a pair of those.

SID If I may say so, Vi…your legs 'ave always looked very nice to me.

VI Alright, alright. Don't give me any soft soap. 'Ow much do you want for the stockings?

SID *(pretending to be offended)* Vi! I'm surprised at you! These is genuine presents from me to you.

VI Well, that's very kind of you Sid, I'm sure.

MUM Very kind. That sugar'll come in 'andy, won't it Vi?

DORIS It's not fair! I've just spent 'alf a week's wages on my stockings and Rose gets them for free.

SID   Ah well, young Doris, you'll 'ave to come to me in future for all your fancies. I'm setting up in business as you might say. Always come to your Uncle Sid first and you won't go far wrong. As I couldn't do my bit on the front line I decided I'd do my bit on the home front instead.

VI   I bet you did. I 'ope this stuff isn't 'ookey.

SID   Vi…Vi..it's straight up, 'onest it is. I've just got my sources, that's all.

(DAD enters with a hammer in his hand)

DAD   Someone will have to come and help me – it's a two handed job this. What's 'e doin' 'ere?

SID   *(reaching in his bag and producing a small packet of tobacco)* I just came to dispense goodwill and cheer, Mr H.

DAD   Oh, ta! Well you can come and help me nail up this blackout stuff then.

SID   Er…I'd like to Mr H. but I've got customers waiting. Can't stop the war effort now, can we?

DAD   Eh?

VI   The girls'll 'elp you Dad. Go on you two. I'll get the tea on the go.

(The girls exit with DAD, arguing about their stockings).

SID   *(Moving over to VI and speaking confidentially)* Now that your Charlie's away, there's no reason why a good looking woman like you should 'ide 'erself away now, is there? Why not come up west with me tonight and 'ave a good time? Strictly pals like. No funny stuff.

VI	I'll get myself a reputation...
SID	No you won't! You and me 'ave known each other a long time, ain't we? In the same class at school an all. You like dancin'. I like dancin'. Be just like brother and sister 'aving a night out. What d'ya say?
VI	Dancing eh? What about your dodgy 'eart?
SID	I'll take me chances. What d'ya say?
VI	Alright. I'll give it a try. No funny stuff though.
SID	Cross me dodgy 'eart. Pick you up at seven, OK?
VI	OK.
SID	See you Ma. Keep up the knitting. What is it anyway?
MUM	It'll be a shroud for you if my Charlie finds out what you're up to.
SID	*(grinning)* See ya. *(SID exits)*
MUM	I 'ope you know what you're doin' Vi...
VI	Oh give over Mum. I 'aven't 'ad a night out since 1937. Even when Charlie was 'ere, 'e never took me dancing. Where's the 'arm? Put the radio on will ya?
	(MUM turns on the radio and there is some dance music playing. VI starts to do a dance round the kitchen table.)
VI	D'you know what Mum? This war might not be so bad after all...
	BLACKOUT. *(Music continues for a while as the actors clear the stage of table and chairs and props.)*
	Lights come up to reveal the two microphones as before. 2nd MAN enters).

2ND MAN   The government didn't build shelters for you. Council workmen just came with a lorry and dumped the bits on your front lawn and left you to get on with it. We didn't think much of the bits, lying out in the rain, gathering rainwater. Just thin bits of corrugated iron, like some old shed. People felt they would be safer in their houses, solid bricks and mortar. They weren't going out in the middle of the night to bury themselves in a grave.

Then my father saw an Anderson that had received a direct hit; he said there was quite a lot of it left; the house it had belonged to was just a heap of bricks.

So he and our neighbour Frank Spedding got cracking. They put me in charge of sorting and counting the bits and pieces while they dug, but I soon got down in the hole. We found old clay pipes and blackened pennies, but only from 1935. Dad said he must have had a hole in his pocket when he was gardening.

Two foot six down, we came across an earthenware pipe running right across the hole. Mr Spedding, who was a builder, said it was a field drain, from the time when our houses were fields. If we dug down through it, all the water in the field, when it rained would end up in our shelter. So they decided to stop digging.

Mr Spedding , being a builder, got all sorts of bits and pieces and we made that shelter a real home from home - we had a stout wooden door and Mr Spedding ran out an electric cable from the house so we had electric light and fire and we used to sit in armchairs making toast.

Then the man came from the council. Nothing was right for

him. We couldn't have a wooden door on the shelter; a bomb would turn it into a mass of splinters and drive them through our flesh as we sat there. We could only have an old blanket over the door. We couldn't have electric light; as a bomb might cut the cable and fry us alive, if the cable touched the metal walls. Worst of all, the shelter should be three feet deep, not two foot six.

Dad told him about the field drain. Dad said he wanted a shelter, not a well for watering the roses. But the man kept waving his little steel ruler and saying that if we didn't put it three feet down, the council would come and take it away, and we could do without.

So we put it down three feet. Dad and Mr Spedding were grim-faced the whole time. Slowly, the shelter filled up with water, like a swimming pool. We did water the roses from it and, in the winter, we sheltered from air raids in the cupboard under the stairs.

(2ND MAN exits and 1ST WOMAN enters with a gas mask over her shoulder)

1ST WOMAN   The one thing we were certain of was that the Germans would use poison gas. Babies had gas masks; horses had gas masks; both were the same size, except the whole baby went inside, but only the horse's head. The baby's mother had to pump air into it, through a concertina thing on the side.

Young children had blue and red ones that looked like Mickey Mouse. Soldiers had very grand hideous ones, with round eyepieces and a long trunk like an elephant. Wardens' were similar, but without the trunk. Ours had a short trunk, and a large window for our eyes. The moment you put it on, the window misted up, blinding you. Our Mums were told to rub soap on the inside of the window, to prevent this. It made it harder to see than ever, and you got soap in your eyes.

There was a rubber washer under your chin, that flipped up and hit you, every time you breathed in. You breathed out with a rude noise echoing round your ears. If you blew really hard, you could make a very rude noise indeed. (You got caned for that during gas practices.) The bottom of the mask soon filled up with spit, and your face got so hot and sweaty you could have screamed.

Once we had our masks tested. We were led through an air raid shelter that the wardens had filled with tear gas. Most of us were alright, but Charlie Blower's mask didn't work. He just sat in class all morning with tears streaming down his face, then the teacher sent him home.

The cardboard boxes that gas masks came in fell apart inside a week. Our Dads bought us long metal cylinders like the German soldiers carried their gas masks in. We used to carry them around on dog leads across our shoulders. These were used in fights. We used to whirl them around our heads, swinging them like swords - they could cut your head open, if you didn't dodge. The guy with the most dented gas mask was the hero. We used to carry bottles of ink and sweets and secret treasures inside. When you had a sudden gas practice, this could be very embarrassing.

(2ND WOMAN enters and 1ST WOMAN stays at her microphone)

2ND WOMAN   Barrage balloons moved into the streets where I lived. We talked to the airmen and airwomen who operated them. The equipment consisted of a large wagon with a winch at the back. This was covered with a cage to protect the operators in case the hawser snapped and whipped back. During bad weather the balloons were brought back to the ground. On more than one occasion I saw balloons that had been cut free. This was done by chopping through the hawser with a sharp axe. In sudden cases of bad weather, or balloons being set on fire by lightning. Sometimes they were set on fire by enemy planes shooting at them. It was very dangerous for people on the ground because the trailing hawser was sometimes dragged across the rooftops, knocking off chimneys and damaging rooftops.

1ST WOMAN   I got to know our local barrage balloon team very well. They were sited on the tennis courts just below our back garden and I spent many hours watching. We occasionally lost a balloon by its breaking free, when it would suddenly shoot up to a tremendous height before drifting away, no doubt to be used as a target for some marauding fighter plane. Alternatively the ears or vanes would tear and, on these occasions, the balloon would go out of control and behave like a demented kite. The crew would try and bring it down but it would tear around on the end of its wire, taking off chimney pots and roofs. On one such occasion the wire crossed the trolley bus cables and disabled all electric transport along the Plumstead road for hours.

(The two WOMEN exit and 1ST MAN enters)

1ST MAN   We never starved, but we ate some very funny things. Best of all was American dried egg. You poured a thin trickle into the frying pan, then as it cooked it blew up like a balloon, till it was two inches thick, like a big yellow humped-back whale.

And we had whale meat, that tasted strongly of fish, unless you soaked it for twenty four hours in vinegar - after which it tasted of vinegar. But there was so much of it. Great big steaks as big as your plate - that we didn't care what it tasted like.

Sausage meat was pale pink. I don't think it had any meat in it at all. Late in the war, my mother got a pound of 'butcher's sausage' - the sausage the butcher made for his own family. It seemed indecent, cos lumps of real meat kept dropping out of it - it nearly made us sick.

I lived a lot on chip butties - but you had to eat them quick before the vinegar reacted with the margarine and turned the chips dark blue.

Our dog helped us out. Our neighbour was on the trawlers and he always reckoned our dog was a good luck mascot. When he went on a trip he would always come and stroke our dog first and when he came back safe he would give the dog a whole pound block of Cadbury's chocolate. The dog used to bring it home in its mouth with half the wrapping chewed off and my mother would immediately requisition it. The number of times we handed round tooth-marked chocolate at Christmas......

(1st MAN exits and 2ND and 3RD WOMEN enter)

3RD WOMAN   As a young girl I loved to go to the dances. I only had two best dance dresses, which I had to alter every now and then to make them look different. We used to get some material or nice paper and fold it carefully to make belts.

We had an open coal fire, but coal was on ration. I can remember Dad going into the woods and chopping down one of the trees so we could have wood for the fire. I thought it was great to see a tree being chopped. My Dad and brother spent all day chopping it up. I can remember my Dad with a wheelbarrow going round the neighbours giving out the logs.

I can remember the excitement on our estate when the Co-op got a box of bananas. Everyone queued up for hours. My mum dragged me to the shop with her. Just one banana and we had to wait all day. I was really bored.

Sometimes the coal ration would run out, so we would put the gas oven on and put our feet inside to keep ourselves warm.

Nobody could afford to make a birthday cake, so instead you had a decorated hatbox as a cake, or a wooden cake with candles on.

2ND WOMAN I had never seen or eaten a banana. Where I lived there was a prisoner of war camp behind us. One day I was walking to the shops when a prisoner called us to the fence and offered my sister, my brother and I three bananas. Not knowing how to eat it, we peeled the banana, ate the skin and threw the inner away.

My father, who was in the Royal Navy, would bring home three pounds of onions when he came on leave. He gave one to my grandmother, one to my mum and one to the priest. The priest would then put them in a raffle and make twenty pounds, which today would be two hundred pounds, just for a few onions.

As there was a great shortage of toys, we played top and whip with a lemonade screw top and a shoelace. My brother had a train set made out of the handle of a brush (that made the coaches and engine), with nailed-on pennies with wheels.

(Both WOMEN exit and THE SINGERS enter and split into two groups. Piano intro and they sing : YES, WE HAVE NO BANANAS!)

YES WE HAVE NO BANANAS! lyrics

SINGERS   There's a fruit store on our street
             It's run by a Greek.
             And he keeps good things to eat
             But you should hear him speak!
             When you ask him anything, he never answers "no".
             He just "yes"es you to death,
             And as he takes your dough, he tells you...
             "Yes! We have no bananas
             We have no bananas today!!
             We have string beans and onions, cabBAges and scallions
             And all kinds of fruit and say
             We have an old fashioned toMAHto
             A Long Island poTAHto, but
             Yes! We have no bananas
             We have no bananas today!"
             Business got so good for him that he wrote home today,
             "Send me Pete and Nick and Jim; I need help right away."

When he got them in the store, there was fun, you bet.

Someone asked for "sparrow grass"

and then the whole quartet All answered:

"Yes, we have no bananas
We have-a no bananas today.

Just try those coconuts
Those wall-nuts and doughnuts
There ain't many nuts like they.

We'll sell you two kinds of red herring,
Dark brown, and ball-bearing.

But yes, we have no bananas
We have no bananas today."

*(THE SINGERS exit. There is a drum roll and 3RD MAN
enters)*

3RD MAN   Liquor is not officially rationed but it often seems as though
it is, since shops handling it won't sell more than a bottle or
so a month to a regular customer and won't sell any at all
to others. There are, of course, good reasons for this.
Distillation of grain for whisky-making was prohibited in
September 1942. Gin, which is manufactured from
imported spirits is in very short supply. Wines are scarce
and, anyhow, so appallingly expensive they are beyond the
average pocket. The demand for beer has accordingly
grown, but a glass of it is often hard to come by – especially
in the country districts whose population has been swelled
by evacuated townsfolk and the military.

Lately there has been a big shortage of beer in London,
which is a big hardship to the working man. Off-licences
have been displaying dummy bottles of liquor in their

windows for so long now that everyone has become used to the pretence. So much so, that recently, my wife stared coldly at a mound of lemons in a greengrocer's window convinced that they were hollow papier-mache mockeries. She discovered later, after they were all gone, that they were part of a crate of the genuine article which had just come in that morning.

(BLACKOUT. Radio music. Stage is set as for previous sketch, with table chairs, radio etc. Music fades. As lights come up MUM and DAD are listening to the radio. A woman's voice is reading out a recipe and MUM is writing it down. DAD is reading a newspaper.)

WOMAN's
VOICE   To make Woolton Pie, dice and cook about one pound each of the following in salted water...

MUM   *(writing)* Salted water...

WOMAN's
VOICE   Potatoes, cauliflower, Swedes, carrots and turnips...

DAD   No bloody meat I s'pose...

WOMAN's
VOICE   Strain but keep three quarters of a pint of vegetable water. Arrange the vegetables in a large pie dish or casserole. Add a little vegetable extract and about one ounce of rolled oats or oatmeal to the vegetable liquid...

DAD   *(with disgust)* Gertcha!

MUM   Shut up Dad!

WOMAN's
VOICE   Cook until thickened and pour over the vegetables. Add

three or four spring onions. Top with potato pastry or with mashed potatoes and a very little grated cheese and heat at the very centre of a moderately hot oven until golden brown. Serve with brown gravy...

MUM   *(writing)* ...brown gravy...

WOMAN's
VOICE   Listen in tomorrow at eight fifteen for the latest recipe from the Kitchen Front – rabbit surprise.

(MUM switches off the radio)

DAD   I bet the surprise is that it's got no bleedin' rabbit in it.

MUM   Oh be quiet Dad. You're not starving yet.

DAD   Not yet, no. If it wasn't for Sid I would be though.

(VI enters, wearing a floral summer dress, with her hair in a matching turban.)

VI   What's that about Sid?

DAD   I was just saying that if it wasn't for Sid, I'd be starving.

MUM   *(pointedly)* Mmm. If it wasn't for Sid, there's a lot of people would 'ave to go without.

VI   *(not rising to the bait)* Very true Mum. Including you. What would you do without Sid, now that they've rationed knitting wool?

MUM   I'm not saying that I'm not grateful. I just think that Sid takes too many liberties, that's all. Mind you, I suppose 'e's encouraged too much, isn't 'e?

DAD   *(not really catching the drift of the conversation)* What are you on about woman?

MUM   Nothing, I'm sure. All I'll say is, there's none so blind as won't see.

DAD   *(to VI)* It's un'inged 'er you know – them rationing knitting
               wool.

MUM   Never thought it would come to that...

VI   Yes, well you've got some now, 'aven't you? Thanks to Sid.

DAD   Anyway. War'll be over soon.

VI   You reckon do you?

DAD   Course it will. Rats leaving the sinking ship. I knew the
               minute that Rudolf 'Ess fella parachuted into Scotland, it
               was the beginning of the end for 'Err 'Itler.

VI   Mmm. I suppose the fact that Germany invaded Russia
               yesterday was just a little mistake was it?

DAD   *(annoyed)* Well yes, my girl, it was, as a matter of fact. Not
               a little mistake – a bloody great big mistake it was. 'E'll
               come unstuck 'e will. Just like Napoleon. The German
               army'll freeze to death in Russia afore them Ruskies give in.
               You see if they don't. Oh yes. 'Err 'Itler's gawn right round
               the bend now.

VI   Well, let's 'ope you're right. Ooh, there's the post.

MUM   Ooh, maybe Charlie's written!

VI   I shouldn't think so Mum. We've 'ad two letters from
               Charlie in two years of war. At this rate 'es not due to write
               until September 1942.

               *(VI exits and returns with four envelopes, three of them
               brown Government letters.)*

MUM   Well perhaps 'e'll get leave soon.

VI	I keep telling you Mum. Charlie don't get leave. 'E's doin' army service instead of a prison sentence. 'E's not allowed 'ome – which suits me fine.
MUM	*(peeved)* Yes I bet it does.
VI	*(calling)* Doris! Rose! Come 'ere quickly! There's something in the post for you!

(She opens up one of the brown envelopes and looks dismayed.)

VI	Oh my Gawd!
MUM	What is it? Is it Charlie?
VI	No it's not Charlie. It's me.
DAD	You?
VI	Yes, me. I've been called up!
MUM and DAD	Called up!
VI	Well, you know, Ministry of Labour. I've got to go and work in munitions.
DAD	Good money in that.
MUM	I thought you was too old.
VI	No. All women between the ages of twenty and fifty. Oh sod it!

(DORIS and ROSE enter. DORIS has been washing her hair and is towelling it.)

ROSE	What is it Mum?
VI	Call up. *(She hands them their envelopes.)* We've all been called up. Munitions.

DORIS	They can't do that! I've already got a job!
VI	Yes they can. Working in a department store is not a reserved occupation.
DORIS	I'm going to look terrible in overalls.
ROSE	*(smugly)* I won't. 'Cos I won't be wearing 'em. *(she waves her letter)* I'm going in the Land Army!
VI	Oh my God!
DORIS	*(enviously)* You jammy beggar!
VI	I don't know what to say. What more can 'appen?
	(At that precise moment SID appears in full uniform. VI screams.)
SID	'Old up! 'Old up! No need to take on. I ain't leavin' for foreign parts y'know.
VI	Sid, you gave me a fright. What you doin' dressed up like that?
SID	'Ome Guard, Vi. I've been conscripted into the 'Ome Guard. I've just come from the kitting out at the Territorial Barracks down Moorfields. We 'aven't actually got any guns yet. They're coming later.
	(DAD gets up and shakes SID's hand.)
DAD	Well done, son. I knew you was a good un.
SID	Thanks. What's to do then? Why the glum faces?
DORIS	Mum and me's been called up to the munitions factory. *(enviously)* Rose is going in the Land Army.
SID	Oh blimey! Well, never mind. Munitions isn't bad. The money's good.

DAD   That's what I said.

SID   'Ere, tell ya what. In 'onour of the occasion, I think I might
                 'ave a little something about my person. *(He gets a half
                 bottle of gin out of his pocket.)*

MUM   Ooh, Mother's Ruin!

VI   Trust you, Sid.

MUM   Is it too early d'you think?

SID   No, Ma. You should either drink gin before breakfast or
                 after it.

                 *(ROSE goes and gets some glasses, DORIS wraps her hair
                 up in the towel. SID pours out some drinks.)*

VI   Oh I forgot the other letter. It's from little Charlie.

DAD   'E ain't so little any more. 'E's fourteen. Time 'e 'ad a job.

VI   Shut up Dad. Listen. *(She takes a swig of her drink and
                 starts to read)* Dear Mum. I 'ad my last day of school today
                 in the village 'all and I'm just writing to ask you if it's
                 alright for me to take a job with the Squire 'ere as under
                 gardener. I 'ave been 'elping Mr Thomas with the garden
                 for some time and Squire 'as offered me a job. 'E says if it's
                 alright with you, I can 'ave it. Bed and board is included, so
                 it means I would be stayin' 'ere and not comin' back to
                 London. Yours sincerely, your son Charlie. Oh bless 'im.

DORIS   Cor. Can't imagine our Charlie digging gardens.

ROSE   No. Nicking the veg more like.

VI   Oy! That's enough of that. That boy 'as changed. You
                 'aven't seen 'im as often as I 'ave. Being in the country's
                 been the best thing for 'im. 'E's settled down. 'E likes it

there and good luck to 'im. I might join 'im meself when this war is over.

DORIS   Ooh not me! I'd die of boredom in the country! 'Ere Rose, do my legs, will'ya?

(DORIS stands up on a chair with her back to the audience and raises her skirt a little. ROSE gets an eyebrow pencil from her pocket and starts to draw a line down the back of each leg.)

DAD   Can't you do that somewhere else? We got company and it ain't decent!

SID   Don't worry about me Mr H. I see all sorts nowadays. 'Ere Vi, ar we still on for Saturday?

VI   I don't know now, Sid. I've got to report to the factory tomorrow and I might be on shift work. 'Ave to play it by ear from now on.

SID   *(disappointed)* Oh yeah, right. 'Ere, what you said about goin' to the country after the war. Did you mean it?

VI   Oh I don't know. I can't see my old man moving out of the smoke.

SID   *(a bit down)* No. I forgot about Charlie.

VI   Still. I don't 'ave to take 'im with me, do I?

SID   *(hopefully)* Don't ya?

VI   Lots of things is going to be different after this war, you mark my words. Lots of things is going to be different.

(BLACKOUT. Music. Table and chairs etc. are removed. When lights come up it is back to the stage with two microphones etc. 3RD MAN enters and goes to a microphone.)

3RD MAN   If Ernest Bevin, the Minister of Labour, has his way, there soon won't be any young girls to take dancing. The call-up of women of twenty and twenty one, along with men of forty and forty one, was announced for next month. The next women to register will be the twenty twos and twenty threes, rather than the eighteens and nineteens, because of the latter's educational commitments. The whole thing has been handled very tenderly. The government has taken into consideration the rooted British antipathy to compulsion of any kind – even in the middle of a life and death struggle. There has been a busy press campaign to assure women that the yellow complexion munitions workers acquired in the last war, when handling TNT, are by no means unavoidable in this one, since science has developed a protective cream which works on all except possessors of ultra-sensitive skin. Nervous parents are also soothed by promises that the State will act as the most vigilant guardians to youthful daughters far from home. Finally, if a woman is pregnant or has young children, she will not be called up at all.

(3RD MAN leaves and 2ND WOMAN enters.)

2ND WOMAN   The part women played in wartime Britain was well illustrated at Listers. Some eight hundred and fifty employees had served in the armed forces by the end of the war, many in the Gloucestershire Regiment and the Royal Gloucestershire Hussars. Some three hundred and fifty women stepped in to carry on the men's work. Listers was the first company to get a sub-factory underway in wartime, when a carpenter's shop and stores were taken over and

converted at Nympsfield. From an initial workforce of eight
local women, who became affectionately known as Nymphs
in 1942, it developed into an all-women sub-factory of
twenty eight. From this small unit, components were
assembled; pipes made; spares for searchlight sets; tanks
landing craft and other wartime ironmongery. Later, the all-
female factory was assembling heavy duty engines. Women
worked a thirty hour week for thirty five shillings –
assembling, brazing and soldering.

The heavy work in munitions earned praise too. In one
works it was reckoned that the women were lifting about
one hundred and eighty gun bodies a day, totalling
something like half a ton in weight. As one joked, "It was
easier work than a hard day doing the family wash!".

(2ND WOMAN exits and 3RD WOMAN enters.)

3RD WOMAN   Tangley Hall Farm on the Burford to Stow road became a
training place for the Land Army and girls were housed in a
hostel at Ducklington. Local people felt sorry for them.
They had come from London – from hairdressers; fashion
shops and beauty parlours – none had got their hands dirty
before. Neither had they ever really got wet and cold
before. The standard Fordson pulling three furrow plough
could be very difficult to start on winter mornings. The
instructor for the girls was a farmer's daughter. They would
plough all day, in any weather. They had poor dinners –
some had flasks but others had nothing to drink all day.
The mimimum rate of pay for the Women's Land Army,
fixed by the Ministry of Agriculture in 1939 was twenty
eight shillings for a forty eight hour week. Where board and

lodging was provided, the recommended charge was fourteen shillings a week.

(3RD WOMAN remains where she is and 1ST WOMAN comes on and takes up position at the opposite microphone.)

1ST WOMAN The national drive to get the public to respond to the War Loan Securities offered in the first three months of the war, exceeded all expectations. Ways to keep the nation investing in the war effort exercised not only the politicians minds but local organisers anxious to get spare pennies out of the public pocket to help their individual campaigns.

The extreme frost that hit the Cotswolds in January 1940 was turned into a fund-raiser, when Earl Bathurst allowed his frozen lake in Cirencester Park to be used for moonlight skating, raising nearly fourteen pounds for the Red Cross Funds. One shilling was charged for skaters and sixpence 'just for looking on.'

The WI held competitions and donated the knitted gloves prize won by Miss Brenda Whiteman to evacuees, then raised their sights to knickers. Funds were set up for cigarettes for the forces. Twelve year old Sylvia Andrews made over fifty knitted doll pincushions which she sold to friends and raised another guinea for the massive Cigarette and Tobacco Fund.

Blood, announced another authority, was the 'best Christmas present you can give'. In an effort to boost the call for good Cotswold blood, it was published that in the first three months Cheltenham had given more of her blood than anywhere else in the region.

It was the hard weaponry of the war machine that really
took hold of the Cotswold imagination though. Knitted
knickers to keep a few bottoms warm, a few gallons of
blood and the transitory comfort of a smoke in the barracks
were one thing; the actual ironmongery that could be hurled
at Hitler and his henchmen were quite another. Nothing
was more popular than the Spitfire Appeal. "Spitfires Up
Nazis Down" Cirencester announced to launch its appeal.
Fairford Spitfire Fund was organized by Mr H.M.Powell
and within two days twenty nine shillings and fivepence had
been collected. Any organisation that raised the five
thousand pounds required to build a Spitfire, had the plane
named after it and took the loss very personally if it was
shot down.

*(Both WOMEN are joined by all the SINGERS, who are
carrying various items – metal pots and pans, old
newspapers, old metal kettles, old flat irons, rubber bicycle
tyres etc. Whatever is appropriate to the next piece. Each
person says a line.)*

EVERYONE   Don't throw anything away, because...

No. 1   Six old bills make one washer for a shell

No. 2   One envelope makes 50 cartridge wads

No. 3   One 9 -inch enamelled saucepan makes a bayonet

No. 4   Two three pint tin kettles make a steel helmet

No. 5   One broken garden fork plus an enamelled pail makes a
tommy-gun

No. 6   Two four inch flat irons make six hand grenades

No. 1   Six and a quarter pounds of rubber makes an airman's

	dinghy
No. 2	Eight and a quarter pounds of rubber makes a Mae West lifejacket
No. 3	One ton of mixed rags makes two hundred and fifty battle dresses and thirteen Army tents
No. 4	Five hundred thousand tons of kitchen waste maintains fifteen thousand pigs.
No. 5	Every pound of bones (except fish bones), after cooking, contains enough fat to provide two ounces of glycerine, which makes double its weight of nitro glycerine, a very high explosive; also two ounces of glue for aircraft work, and the rest is ground down for feeding stuffs for animals and poultry.
EVERYONE	*(Shouting)* DON'T THROW ANYTHING AWAY!

BLACKOUT.

END OF ACT I

ACT TWO

(Blackout. The stage setting remains the same. MUSIC – "The Yanks Are Coming". During the blackout an American flag comes down to hang over the central flat which shows the image of a radio. Lights come up. 1ST MAN enters and goes to a microphone. MUSIC fades.)

1ST MAN   'Japanese planes have attacked Pearl Harbour.' I spent the whole weekend in a daze. Then Hitler declared war on America and I knew he was mad. And America became magic! The things we heard of! Bulldozers that could build a whole airfield in twenty four hours. Liberty ships built in a week, from the first plate being laid. The Americans were going to build twenty five thousand planes a year...there had only been three thousand on both sides in the Battle of Britain. The war had become, as we soon learnt to say, 'a different ball game.'

American comics flooded in : new heroes like Superman and Dick Tracy, the cop with the two-way wrist TV and a nose like a rectangular kite. And jazz records we learned to listen to in the American way - heads neck-breakingly on one side, nodding wisely in time with the music, clicking our fingers to the rhythm and, if possible, chewing gum. They seemed to be all about travel these records. We were urged to 'Take the A train' or the 'Chatanooga Choo Choo', especially on 'Route 66', Americans always seemed to be arriving or departing.

We learnt that Betty Grable had the best legs in the world

and had them insured for a million dollars (the word 'million' was on everyone's lips). Better still, she was married to Harry James, who could play 'The Flight of the Bumble Bee' on the trumpet, faster than it had ever been played before.

Our other hero was Fats Waller, the huge negro who invented Boogie Woogie. Every kid who was allowed near a piano could play the left-hand roll of Boogie Woogie.

The Yanks were tops. The American aeroplanes had much more exciting names, even swearing names, like the Grumman Hellcat.

I made an impassioned speech in our school debating society, about the superiority of all things American. My beloved English teacher seemed a little distant... I couldn't understand it - I'd always been one of his favourites before that...

(1ST MAN exits and 2ND MAN enters.)

2ND MAN   After America entered the War, the American public swept aside all its previously-held prejudices against servicemen, and the uniform became a symbol of pride. Girls flocked to soldiers, sailors, airmen and marines. The marriage rates soared. In the first five months after Pearl Harbour, an estimated one thousand women a day married servicemen. Some of the quickie marriages involved unscrupulous women known as 'Allotment Annies'. After marrying, they received the fifty dollars monthly allotment cheque due to each serviceman's wife and were the beneficiaries of the GI's ten thousand dollar life-insurance policy. Some married more than one GI at a time. One Allotment Annie specialized in combat pilots, who were known to have a high mortality rate. Another woman, who was only seventeen, worked as a hostess in a nightclub and specialized in sailors who shipped out from the big Naval base at Norfolk, Virginia. Two of her husbands met by chance at a pub in England and compared pictures of their wives. After the Shore Patrol broke up the fight, the two sailors joined forces to end the career of that particular Annie.

(2ND MAN exits and 1ST WOMAN enters)

1ST WOMAN To the general atmosphere of watchful waiting has been added the impatience of the American Troops now in London, most of whom talk as though they were somewhat doubtful of being able to give the town a quick once-over before leaving for a date with von Runstedt, which they seem to imagine will be around Thursday week at the latest. Any Canadians who happen to be present when this little jaunt is outlined usually smile with the weary irony of men who thought much the same thing two years and several hundred pints of English-village beer ago.

The newspapers have dutifully been giving their readers stories about the American troops who arrived the other day and have caused an unprecedented scarcity of taxis throughout the metropolis.

Lists of 'do's' and 'don'ts' have been issued for the benefit of hospitable Britons who want to ask the boys home. DON'T mention the tardiness of the United States in entering the war. Motherly ladies who might want to get out the best tea service for their uniformed visitors are warned that most Americans DON'T look upon tea as a customary afternoon rite. At the same time, British householders are told that they had better not produce their precious monthly ration of whisky, as the guests are liable to knock it off blithely at one sitting, without realizing that it's hard to come by in England nowadays.

For all the 'do's' and 'don'ts', Anglo American relations still seem fine.

(1ST WOMAN exits and AMERICAN SOLDIER enters)

AMERICAN
SOLDIER

I came to Wotton-under-Edge with the 45th American Evacuation Hospital on 25th November 1943. Many of us had never been away from our homes before and we wondered what England would be like. I was with a friend in the town when we met a girl named Betty, who had come down the hill to do some shopping and we asked her if she could show us a little of the town. She told us to wait while she went to get some bread for the weekend. But when she returned without any, we realized how you nice English people were short of food with everything so tightly rationed. We then asked Betty to wait a while and we got her a nice big loaf from our American stores. She was so grateful and asked us home to meet her parents. That started a friendship that was to last for many years.

I had my first fish and chips in Wotton-under-Edge. We couldn't understand what was going on when they put the fish and chips in paper and we started laughing. I guess the Cotswold folk had a laugh out of us too, because we didn't know what they meant by 'Q-up' - but we soon found out when we didn't stand in line and wait our turn.

(AMERICAN SOLDIER exits and 3RD MAN (in British uniform enters.)

3RD MAN   It was the arrival of the Americans in August 1942 which caused the greatest stir; hardly a village or hamlet had not hosted one unit or other of the armed forces by then. Khaki blended in with the countryside and heavy armoured vehicles churned up country lanes. But the rapture for welcoming the heroes was reserved for the slickly uniformed Americans and they were greeted with the euphoria of a liberating force when they sailed into Avonmouth and into the West Country. Three long years of war, miserly pay and blitz weary, the Tommy, in his coarse cloth uniform merged even further into the background with his Brylcream and Woodbines as the Yanks swept the local girls off their feet, literally, with the uninhibited jiving, the smooth cloth uniform that had not seen the dust of active duty on it and deodorized bodies unstained by the sweat of fight and fear. Lucky Strike cigarettes made the little Woodbine look weedy in comparison, and sharing two ounces of humbugs on the barrack room bench hauled into the village hall to watch a jerky film, transmitted through a beam of thick smoke from a gyrating projector which frequently broke down, was a primitive pastime when the Yanks had money to take girls to the proper 'flicks.' Lavish with compliments and candy, nylons and other niceties of which the local people had been starved for three years, the American troops appeared as film stars from the land of plenty. 'Gum' and 'gas' became synonymous with GI's. Not unnaturally the local boys and English servicemen resented the invasion of their transatlantic cousins and girls who dated Yanks became known as 'Spam-bashers' or 'Yankee bashers' and other unrepeatable names.

(3RD MAN exits and 2ND WOMAN enters. Sounds of bombing are heard.)

2ND WOMAN   My father came off duty looking pale and sick, and said the Germans had scored a direct hit on Wilkinson's Lemonade Factory, and hundreds had been killed, and some were still trapped down in the cellars. He said there should never have been a shelter down there. There'd been heavy bottling machinery on the ground floor, just standing on wooden boards, and when the bomb hit, it all just collapsed on the people below.

Terrible rumours started going around. People so crushed they couldn't be recognized; people sitting down there without a mark on them, just dead. Mothers with babies in their arms. A man still holding his accordion...

Everybody was stunned; couldn't cope. Why had God let it happen?

Then the stories changed. Wicked things had gone on in that shelter. People had taken drink down there and held parties. Music and dancing every night. Immorality and they didn't care who saw it...People went there even when there wasn't a raid going on. Gambling...

People said it was a judgement. God is not mocked. It was like Sodom and Gomorrah.

Everybody felt much better after that.

(Blackout. MUSIC: Workers Playtime. Stage is set up with table and chairs etc. After a few bars of the Music there is then the sound of bombing, fades as lights come up. It is about five o'clock in the morning. VI has come off shift at the factory and is sitting at the kitchen table.

She is wearing dungarees and her hair is in a turban. She is having a cup of tea and reading a magazine. Suddenly there is a racket at the front door. DORIS and ROSE are giggling and saying "ssh". They appear with two AMERICAN SOLDIERS - one middle aged and one very young.)

VI   *(not really looking up from her magazine)* What sort of time do you call this? And whose that with you?

GEORGE   Gee, we're sorry ma'am. No offence meant...

                (VI leaps up from the table and looks embarrassed.)

VI   No. no, that's alright. I'm sorry I must look a mess, I've just come home from the factory.

DORIS   I thought your shift didn't finish until six Mum?

VI   Yes I can see that. Thought you'd be able to slip in before I got home didn't you and I wouldn't know that you'd been out all night.

ROSE   We couldn't help it mum, we got stuck down the shelter all night. They've only just sounded the all clear.

VI   Yes I know. That's why I'm home early. The factory was hit.

                (Both girls rush to her realising that she looks a bit distressed.)

DORIS   Are you alright mum?

VI	Yes. I'm alright, don't fuss. They got the casings section. There was a big fire so they sent us home.
ROSE	Were there any...
VI	Yes. Fifty four killed at last count. There may be more.
GEORGE	Gee. I'm sorry. Look we'd better go...
VI	No! No, please. Where's my manners. Introduce your friends girls. I'll put the kettle on.
GEORGE	Er. I've got something stronger ma'am. You look as though you could do with it. *(He holds out a bottle.)*
DORIS	This is George, mum.
VI	Hello George, I'm Vi.
GEORGE	Please to meet you VI. This is a bottle of pure Kentucky bourbon and this young man here is my good friend Joe.
JOE	Howdy ma'am.
GEORGE	I'm looking after Joe, you might say, on account of his being a backwoods boy still wet behind the ears.
	(DORIS and ROSE giggle and JOE hangs his head in embarrasment.)
ROSE	We got stuck down the Aldwych tube station when the sirens started and that's where we met George and Joe.
VI	Well take a seat George and Joe and let's see what that booze of yours is like.
GEORGE	Yes ma'am.
VI	Please call me Vi. Ma'am makes me sound like the Queen.
GEORGE	Be a pleasure Vi.

ROSE	*(fetching glasses)* George has a big ranch near Chicago, mum.
VI	*(taking it with a pinch of salt)* Well I never. You're the tenth Yank I've met with a big ranch. Doesn't anyone live in normal houses in America?
JOE	I do ma'am.
GEORGE	Yes ma'am – sorry Vi. This boy lives in a shack with no running water or electricity. Why his folks are dirt poor. First pair of boots he's ever had were given to him by the army.
VI	*(interested)* Really, I never knew that there were poor people in America. I thought you were all rich. Well, rich compared to us that is.
JOE	No ma'am. But I will be rich, when the war's over. I'm gonna get a job in the big city.
GEORGE	There you are Vi. The old American pioneer spirit. Why this boy may be dirt poor now but who knows? In twenty years time he could be President!
VI	Fancy that. What do you call this booze?
GEORGE	Bourbon.
VI	Funny taste. But it warms you up a treat.
DORIS	Course, we're all gonna be well off in Britain now.
VI	We are?
DORIS	Yes. The Beveridge Report.
VI	Oh that.
GEORGE	What's the Beveridge Report little ladies?

VI	A plan for social security. The Government's going to look after us all in our old age. If we ever reach old age that is.
ROSE	Yeah. For two bob a week we get a guaranteed pension when we get old. Not bad eh? My grandad can't stop talking about it. 'E says we're going to get free spectacles and teeth next.
DORIS	Who wants 'em?!
ROSE	*(sniggering)* Grandad does, silly!
GEORGE	Gee, it sounds like the British could teach the Americans a few lessons.
VI	*(she is getting a little drunk)* Won't do the poor sods who copped a bomb today any good though will it?
GEORGE	Hey, hey! Steady with that bourbon Vi. You haven't had anything to eat I bet.
	How about some of this?
	(He gets bars of chocolate out of his pocket. The women stare in disbelief.)
DORIS	I haven't seen chocolate for three years...
ROSE	Chocolate...
VI	Bloody hell...
GEORGE	Go ahead...
	(The women pounce on the bars, unwrap them and stuff the chocolate in their mouths. They make noises of ecstasy, GEORGE and JOE start smiling, the women start giggling.)
VI	*(raising her glass)* God Bless America!
GEORGE	I'll drink to that Vi....

(Just then SID's voice calls out "It's only me" and he enters)

SID   I brought you some eggs.... Oh bit early for company isn't
             it? *(He looks a bit put out.)*

VI   Come in Sid. Meet George and Joe. The girls brought them
             home this morning. They've just been cheering us up with
             some...bourbon?..

GEORGE   Bourbon...

VI   And some chocolate *(she holds up the chocolate with a big
             smile)*   ·

             (SID shakes hands with the Yanks a bit reluctantly)

SID   Well, that makes my eggs look a bit poor doesn't it?

VI   Oh shut up Sid *(she kisses his cheek which cheers him up)*
             Sit down and have some bourbon and I'll make us all some
             breakfast.

SID   Alright.

DORIS   Mum's factory got bombed last night Sid.

SID   *(leaping up in alarm)* Vi! I didn't know! Are you alright?

VI   I'm fine, I'm fine, don't fuss. In fact I'm beginning to feel
             quite good now.

GEORGE   Bourbon 'll do it every time...

SID   *(taking a sip and not liking it)* Eugh! You must be joking
             George old man. This stuff is not a patch on Scotch
             Whisky.

             (SID produces a half bottle of scotch and the girls whoop.)

GEORGE   Oh, oh, oh, Sid old bean. I can do even better than that.
             (He produces a hip flask, unscrews the top and wafts it

under Sid's nose.) A drop of the Irish huh?

SID   Ah, now you're talking my son...

(Everyone starts to chatter and laugh amongst themselves. There is a knock at the front door and VI goes to answer it. The pleasant mood continues until, a few seconds later, VI comes back into the room clutching a telegram. She stands in a state of shock until SID notices her and, as he stands he alerts the two girls. Everyone falls silent and looks at VI.)

SID   What is it Vi?

VI   *(very slowly as if not quite believing it)* It's Charlie. He's....he's been ...killed. In...North Africa...

(The girls start to cry very quietly.)

GEORGE   *(To JOE)* C'mon son, we'd better go and leave these good people to their grief.

SID   Yes. Thanks mates. I'll show you out.

GEORGE   *(stopping at VI and taking her hand)* I'm so sorry Vi.

VI   *(hugging him and JOE)* You take care of yourselves won't you.

JOE   We will ma'am.

(SID takes the two Yanks out. DORIS and ROSE put their arms around each other for comfort and go out crying quietly. VI goes and sits at the table. She still hasn't cried. SID comes back in.)

SID   Do you want me to go and wake Mr H and Ma?

VI   No, let them sleep. Time enough to tell them the bad news.

SID   I'm sorry Vi. I...don't know what to say...

VI   Neither do I Sid, neither do I. I mean there was no love lost
        between Charlie and me, you know that.

SID   I know he never treated you right Vi.

VI   He just wouldn't give up thieving. Three times inside and
        he still couldn't see it was a mugs game. He wasn't
        interested in me or the kids. He just wanted to be king of
        the heap - jack the lad. What his mates thought of him
        mattered more than anything else. He was weak and there
        were times I hated him. But, as God is my witness Sid, I
        never wished him dead.

SID   I know you didn't Vi.

VI   And now he's gone and I hope he got a bloody medal for it.
        That would be nice. Something good to leave after him.
        Let's have a drink.

        (*She pours SID and herself a drink and raises her glass.*)

        Here's to Charlie. May he rest in peace.

SID   (*raising his glass*) To Charlie.

        (*Blackout. MUSIC : "I'll remember you". Table, chairs and
        props are cleared. Music fades and then the sound of
        a V1 rocket buzzing, stopping and an explosion. Lights
        come up and the American flag is gone. It has been replaced
        by a large London Underground symbol. 3RD WOMAN
        enters and reds from a paper.*)

3RD WOMAN If history is being torn up by the roots in London, history is
        also being made. The new race of tube dwellers is slipping a

fresh page into the record: nothing has ever been seen like the concourse of humanity that camps underground every night. As early as eleven thirty in the morning, people start going down to stake out the evening's claim with folded rugs, newspapers, or bundles of bedding. By five, when the homeward rush hour is on, one walks underground between double rows of men, women and children - eating, drinking, sleeping, reading newspapers and just sitting ; all part of the most extraordinary mass picnic the world has ever known.

The tubes are so much home to them now that they take off their shoes and stockings, loosen their collars, feed their babies, and carry on their personal quarrels without seeming to be any more aware of the tramp of passing feet than one is of traffic in a busy street. The authorities are working out a system of permanent canteens, and have also talked about compulsory innoculations and disinfectant sprays, as an epidemic of influenza - if nothing worse - would seem to be inevitable when the bad weather sets in and people go straight down off the streets in their wet clothes.

(3RD WOMAN exits and 2ND WOMAN enters and reads from a paper.)

2ND WOMAN On Friday, Hitler's secret weapon had stopped being a rumour and the butt of jokes when there was a sudden attack on Southern England by pilotless planes. People know that the pilotless planes can't affect the outcome of the Battle of Normandy one jot but they are also resigned to the fact that it may easily make life here uncomfortable and hazardous in a new sort of way. What principally bothers the southern English at this moment is a certain illogical Wellsian creepiness about the idea of a robot skulking about overhead, in place of merely a young Nazi with his finger on the bomb button.

Mothers are despatching delighted youngsters to school these days with instructions for them to duck into the nearest doorway should they see an odd-shaped, winged missile which, reportedly, hums like a motorbike and is lit up at the tail and otherwise carries on suspiciously.

(2ND WOMAN exits and 3RD MAN enters)

3RD MAN   At the moment, children are again a major problem to the London authorities, for, however stirring the news may be from other battlefronts, the battle of London is still grim. For some reason, many parents who, ages ago, sent their children away to safe billets have decided that the war news is good enough to warrant bringing them back. In spite of Mr Churchill's plain speaking and the plain evidence of the robot rockets, some cockneys seem convinced that a dead Londoner is better any day than a live yokel. The newspapers are waging a campaign to get the children who are still here to leave and the ones who have already gone away to stay put. In a story about a hundred and forty nine children who hadn't been evacuated from one school, the Daily Herald referred to them as one hundred and forty nine candidates for crippledom. Possibly the unpopular business called compulsion is the only thing that will do the trick.

(3RD MAN stays where he is. All others (MEN, WOMEN and SINGERS but not the family,) come on to the stage.

Two of them are wearing hard hats and ARP warden
armbands.)

1ST WOMAN   Prime Minister Churchill's statement, which made it alright
            to talk out loud about V2's instead of cautiously referring
            to it as if it were something supernatural which had
            dropped in somehow and made a big hole in the back yard,
            came as a relief to the inhabitants of southern England. The
            Government's secrecy and the ordinary public's silence since
            the first of those new things arrived have both been amazing.

2ND MAN   The new bombs had been expected for so long that by the
            time they did turn up a lot of people here had reached a
            state of scepticism and for a while they thought the distant,
            unheralded explosions were anything from a stray robot
            rocket to a thunderstorm. Even when it became apparent
            that the V2 was a reality, nobody mentioned the thing by
            name in public.

2ND WOMAN Perhaps because of the deliberately planted rumours, the
           first big, mysterious explosion was ascribed to a bursting
           gas main, and that fiction was solemnly maintained for days
           until someone said it was extraordinary how many gas
           mains had been going up lately.

3RD MAN   Now that the secret is out, the great question is whether the
            V2 is worse than the VI. Jumpy folk are inclined to believe
            that they prefer the VI because it could at least be detected
            by the defenses in time to sound a warning. The V2, with
            nasty abruptness, just arrives. "If I'm going to be killed"
            one lady remarked "I would like to have the excitement of
            knowing it's going to happen."

            (Blackout, then there are sounds of bombing, then an

*almighty explosion. The lights go up to reveal MUM and
DAD sitting in the middle of a bare stage on top of some
debris surrounded by odd items that they have salvaged
from the wreckage of their house. MUM is dressed in her
nightdress, with her coat over the top. She has rags in her
hair. DAD is dressed in pyjamas with a cardigan over the
top and a flat cap. MUM talks inanely. DAD stares into
space.)*

MUM   I don't expect she'll be long now...they'll 'ave 'ad to find 'er
in the factory.

(Silence)

Oh look, there's Mrs Williams. I'm glad she got out alright.
I was worried about 'er, cos she's got such bad legs, she
wouldn't 'ave been able to run very fast. She's saved 'er
pickled eggs I see.That's good. She's been pickling them eggs
for over a year now and she always said to me, she said
"Elsie, if I go, you make sure you take them pickled eggs. I
don't want her from No.42 getting 'er 'ands on 'em." *(She
waves to an unseen Mrs Williams)* Oo-oo! Got yer eggs
then? ....Good.

(Silence)

I feel lost without some knitting to do. I say, Dad, I said I
feel lost without some knitting to do.

(No response from DAD.)

Still...at least I've still got me needles. *(She holds up two
knitting needles which are blackened and bent out of shape)*

You'll 'ave to straighten them out for me, Dad.

(Silence)

Ah well...the war'll be over this time next week...so they say...

(DAD finally responds by turning round to glare at her.)

DAD   Oh they say that do they?

MUM   Yes. Course they do. They said on the radio last night that our boys had crossed the Rhine and were advancing on Berlin. They said it was all over bar the shouting.

DAD   *(shouting)* Then would someone mind telling the stupid Nazi bastard who just sent that V bomb over that wiped our bloody street out!!!

MUM   Dad! Language!

DAD   The war'll be over this time next week... Wake up woman! This bloody war is never going to end!

MUM   *(sniffing)* Dad...you're just upset...

DAD   Upset?! Course I'm bloody upset! I've just 'ad my 'ome blown to smithereens. Bloody pub's gone too. I can't even drown me sorrows. But you're alright. You've got your bloody knitting needles. Churchill can sleep safe in 'is bed knowing that it ain't gonna be long afore you start bloody knitting again!

(VI enters in a rush.)

VI   Oh there you are. Thank goodness you're alright. My stomach turned right over when I saw the warden come towards me in the factory.

MUM   Thank Gawd you've come Vi. It's been terrible. The whole street's gone...

VI   I know. It's been a bad night all round Mum. I 'ope Doris is

	alright. Thank God the other two are in the country.
DAD	What about Sid?
VI	I've sent a message to Sid, Dad. 'E's manning the anti-aircraft gun on 'Ampstead 'Eath tonight. E'll get 'ere when 'e can.
DAD	*(muttering)* I've got to see Sid.
MUM	Dad's upset. The bomb got the pub too.
VI	*(understanding)* I see. Don't worry Dad. Sid's always got a bottle with 'im. Mum, 'ave you 'ad a cup of tea?
MUM	No love. We've not 'ad anything. Everyone's been very kind but they've been so busy and we didn't like to ask.
DAD	*(grimly)* Look at that over there. No.54. The O'Reilly kids. All five of them. Dead. She should 'ave evacuated 'em long ago.

(SID enters)

VI	Oh Sid - thank God you're 'ere. *(she hugs him)* The whole street got wiped out. 'Ave you got a drink for Dad?
SID	Course I 'ave. 'Ere'y'are Dad. *(He hands over a hip flask.)*.
DAD	Thanks son. I need this.
SID	You'll all 'ave to come and stay with me now, Vi. I won't 'ave any argument.
MUM	Mrs 'Astings says that 'er family's going to get one of them nice new prefabs they're putting up over Newington Green way. I wouldn't mind one of them. They got all mod cons you know.
VI	We'll see Mum. I just want to 'ave a word with Sid for a minute, alright?

MUM	Yes ducks, don't mind us.

(VI takes SID to one side.)

VI	Oh this is bloody typical isn't it. My family cops it just as the war is coming to an end...
SID	Now then Vi. You got a lot to be grateful for. Everyone's alive.
VI	Yes you're right....*(pause)* Sid..you must have made a pretty penny out of your black market dealings, I bet.
SID	I'm alright. Whatever I got you can 'ave Vi, you know that.
VI	You're OK Sidney Potts. At first I thought you was just like my Charlie, God rest 'is soul...just another chiselling no-good on the make all the time. But you've stuck by me and my family, which is a lot more than Charlie ever done.
SID	You know 'ow I feel about you, Vi.
VI	Right. So I'm gonna make you a proposition Sid. There's this this little shop in the country, near where my son is living, that's comin' up for rent.

Now, 'ow about we take that money of yours and we get this shop. Get out of London altogether. Make a fresh start eh? Course, we'll 'ave to take Mum and Dad with us, but they won't be any bother. Doris won't leave London but I reckon she's old enough to fend for 'erself. Rose – well I don't know what she'll do. If I know 'er, she'll be off to America as a GI bride when this war is over. So what d'ya say? I'll take some time off work, on account of being homeless, I'll pop down to the country and sort out the shop. You can go round to get a special licence. We can get married the day after and then get the old folks settled in the new place.

Eh?

SID   *(flabbergasted)*   I..I..don't know what to say...

DAD   Say yes, you daft bugger, then we can all get out of 'ere.

SID   Yes!

VI   *(hugging him)* The war'll be over soon and there'll be nothing 'ere for the likes of us. I reckon we should leave London to the youngsters, they've got the energy to rebuild it. I want a bit of peace and quiet now.

MUM   Vi?

VI   Yes Mum?

MUM   When Sid comes down off cloud nine...ask 'im if 'e could get me a new pair of knitting needles would ya?

              (ARP WARDEN enters.)

WARDEN   Just to let you know, the doctor's coming down the road if you need him. And the tea wagon is on its way.

MUM   Oh thank Gawd! I'm gaspin' for a cup of tea.

              (Various people come on stage. A lady with a tea urn, cups and saucers on a trolley, a man with his head bandaged and being helped by a nurse, a couple of soldiers with shovels in their hands ready to dig through the rubble etc. A man sits down and begins to play a melancholy song on a mouth organ.)

DAD   'Ere, mate – not wishing to be disrespectful like, but could you play somethin' a bit more cheerful? Something we could sing along to?

MAN   'Ow about this? *(He plays a few bars of "Roll out the Barrel" and everyone joins in.)*

ROLL OUT THE BARREL - lyrics

EVERYONE   Roll out the barrel, We'll have a barrel of fun

               Roll out the barrel, we've got the blues on the run

               Zing Boom Terrara

               Join in a glass of good cheer

               Now it's time to roll the barrel

               For the gang's all here

               (Repeat)

               (Halfway through the repeat an air raid siren sounds.)

SID   O Blimey! 'Ere we go again! *(shouting)* Everyone down the shelters! Come on!

WARDEN   Oy! That's my job! *(shouting)* Everyone down the shelters! Come on! Hurry up!

               (Everyone exits. BLACKOUT. Siren stops. MUSIC. Lights go up. Curtain Call.)

FURNITURE LIST (for review)

Two 1940s style radio microphones on opposite sides of the stage.

ACT 1:	Large image of 1940s style radio, upstage centre.
ACT II:	Large American flag, upstage centre.
ACT II:	Page 48. American flag replaced by large image of London Underground symbol, upstage centre.

FURNITURE LIST (for sketches)

Page 8 :	Actors bring on small wooden table and four chairs during blackout. Furniture is removed on page 14.
Page 23:	Same as for page 8. Furniture is removed on page 29.
Page 41:	Same as for page 8. Furniture is removed on page 47.
Page 51:	A couple of broken chairs and other "bomb damaged" furniture can be brought onstage during the blackout. Stays on until the end of the play.

PROPERTY LIST

Page 7:	Radio needs to be placed on table, also teapot and cups.
	MUM has knitting needles and wool.
Page 8:	DORIS enters with two pairs of stockings.
Page 10:	SID enters with a large canvas shoulder bag containing a bag of sugar (brown paper wrapping), three pairs of stockings and a packet of tobacco.
Page 13:	DAD enters with a hammer.
Page 14:	ALL PROPS AND FURNITURE CLEARED FROM STAGE.
Page 16:	1ST WOMAN enters with a gas mask in its case, over her shoulder.
Page 23:	Radio on table. MUM needs a pencil and paper and her usual knitting needles and wool. Teapot and teacups on table.
	DAD needs a newspaper.
Page 25:	VI exits and returns with three brown envelopes and one white envelope.
Page 26:	DORIS enters with a towel. ROSE has an eyebrow pencil in her pocket.
Page 27:	SID enters with half a bottle of gin in his pocket.
Page 28:	ROSE exits and returns with six glasses on a tray.
Page 29:	ALL PROPS AND FURNITURE CLEARED FROM STAGE.
Page 33:	All the review actors and singers come onstage with various items (as per script) – bills; envelopes; enamelled saucepan; two tin kettles; one garden fork; two flat irons; rubber; rags; kitchen waste in a tin bucket; bones.
Page 41:	Radio, teapot, cups, glasses on table. VI is reading a magazine.
	GEORGE enters carrying a bottle of bourbon. He also has bars of chocolate in his pocket and a hip flask.

Page 45:   SID enters with a box of eggs and he has half a bottle of
                Scotch in his pocket.

Page 46:   VI exits and returns with a telegram.

Page 47:   ALL PROPS AND FURNITURE CLEARED FROM STAGE.

Page 51:   "bomb debris" is required. Just a couple of broken chairs;
                a blackened kettle; some clothes/rags strewn about. MUM
                has two bent and blackened knitting needles.

Page 53:   SID enters. He has a hip flask in his pocket.

Page 55:   lady enters with a tea urn, cups and saucers on a trolley.

                Two soldiers carrying shovels; a man with a mouth organ.

                Other members of the cast can carry on props if required.
                Things they have salvaged from the bombing.

LIGHTING AND EFFECTS

To start:

Spotlights on each radio microphone and on the upstage centre image of a radio.

SFX: "V for Victory" drumbeat.

General lighting comes up.

The SINGERS enter and the intro is played for "There'll always be an England", then the accompaniment for the full song.

Page 3:

CUE: 1ST WOMAN: "As unreal as the popular songs on the wireless..."

SFX: Intro to "The Seigfried Line", then accompaniment to full song.

Page 5:

CUE: 3RD WOMAN: "...be the beginning of a serious back-to-the-land movement?"

SFX : A few bars of "Stars and Stripes Forever" – fade as AMERICAN REPORTER takes up position at microphone.

Page 7:

CUE: AMERICAN REPORTER: "So folks, please remember, your friends in America do care."

SFX: A few bars of "Stars and Stripes Forever", then...

Lighting: blackout.

SFX: "Stars and Stripes" continues for a few moments then is faded. VOICE OF WINSTON CHURCHILL is played.

Page 8:

CUE: VOICE OF WINSTON CHURCHILL: "The whole fury and might of the enemy must very soon be turned on us."

Lighting: bring up general lighting.

CUE: VOICE OF WINSTON CHURCHILL: "This was their final hour."

SFX : National Anthem plays.

CUE: VI switches off the radio.

SFX: *National Anthem stops.*

Page 14:   CUE: VI: "Put the radio on will ya?" MUM switches on radio.

SFX: *dance music plays.*

CUE: VI: "This war might not be so bad after all…"

Lighting: blackout continues until stage is cleared.

SFX: dance music continues throughout blackout, then fades as…

Lighting : general lighting comes up.

Page 21:   CUE: 2ND WOMAN: "…with nailed on pennies for wheels."

SFX Intro is played for "Yes, We Have No Bananas" followed by full accompaniment.

Page 22:   CUE: The SINGERS exit.

SFX: *A drum roll.*

Page 23:   CUE: 3RD MAN: "…which had just come in that morning."

Lighting: blackout which continues until stage is set.

SFX: radio dance music plays until stage is set, then it fades and WOMAN's VOICE on the radio takes over.

CUE: WOMAN's VOICE: "To make Woolton Pie…"

Lighting: general lighting comes up.

Page 29:   CUE: VI: "Lots of things is going to be different."

Lighting: blackout, which continues until set is cleared.

SFX: Radio music, which continues until stage is cleared.

Lighting: general lighting comes up when 3RD MAN enters.

Page 34:   CUE : EVERYONE: "DON'T THROW ANYTHING
                  AWAY!"

                  Lighting: blackout then house lights.

                  SFX: Interval music.

START OF ACT II

                  Lighting : blackout.

                  *SFX: Music "The Yanks Are Coming" which plays for a
                  couple of minutes, then...*

                  Lighting: Lights come up.

                  SFX: Music fades.

Page 41:   CUE: 2ND WOMAN: "Everybody felt much better after
                  that."

                  Lighting : blackout until stage is set.

                  *SFX: Music "Worker's Playtime" which plays for about 30
                  seconds and is then replaced by sounds of bombing and
                  anti-aircraft guns.*

                  Lighting: general lighting comes up.

                  SFX: sounds of bombing fade.

Page 47:   CUE: SID: "To Charlie."

                  Lighting: blackout which lasts until stage is cleared.

                  *SFX: Music "I'll Remember You, Always", which fades
                  when stage is cleared to be replaced by the sound of a V1
                  rocket.*

                  Once the explosion has happened then...

Lighting: general lighting comes up.

Page 51:   CUE: 3RD MAN: "…the excitement of knowing it's going to Happen."

Lighting: blackout until stage is set.

SFX: sounds of bombing (about 30 seconds) followed by one large explosion.

Lighting: general lights go up again.

Page 55:   CUE: various people come on stage. MAN begins to play mouth organ.

SFX : if the mouth organ is being provided by technicians, and the actor is miming, then the first piece should be mournful.

Page 56:   CUE: DAD: "Ere mate…"

SFX: mouth organ music stops.

CUE: MAN: "Ow about this?"

SFX : a few bars of "Roll Out The Barrel" which continues as everyone sings, then is broken into, halfway through the repeat by an air-raid siren, which continues until…

CUE: WARDEN: "Hurry up!"

Lighting: blackout.

SFX: Siren is replaced by music.

Lighting: stage and house lights up. Curtain calls.